Beneath Occluded Shine

poems by

Claudia M. Stanek

Finishing Line Press
Georgetown, Kentucky

Beneath Occluded Shine

ACKNOWLEDGMENTS

Grateful acknowledgment is given to the following where these poems first
appeared:

Modern Poetry Quarterly Review—"Transparent Language"
Bitterzoet—"Family History" and "Sunday Morning in Broken November"
Poetry Society of Tennessee Anthology 2023—"Hands Full of Heaven"
Ruminate—"Smoke and Cloud"

Publisher: Leah Huete de Maines
Editor: Christen Kincaid
Cover Art: Jules Nyquist
Author Photo: Kara Hudgens
Cover Design: Elizabeth Maines McCleavy

Order online: www.finishinglinepress.com
also available on amazon.com

Author inquiries and mail orders:
Finishing Line Press
PO Box 1626
Georgetown, Kentucky 40324
USA

Contents

Transparent Language

Is it true they scatter
transparent letters across the sky?
            Neruda

When you raise your eyes
to the punctuated sky, you see
letters of all scripts, scattered
in mock collage.

When you shield your eyes
from the glory of the sun, you see
the random spatter of the words
that matter most on your palm.

When your eyes no longer see
anything but a mist of light,
the magnifier that should illumine
sentences will brand your hand.

When you wish you had never
known sight, you will listen
for transparent clauses
but hear the lonely Braille of "I."

Sunday Morning in Broken November

How long do others speak
If we have already spoken?
Neruda

Sabbath morning rakes
my skin as I tour
St. Mary's to learn
how the names of dead
Poles speak.
Headstones shiver
as I photograph rows
of silent "ski's" and
"wicz's. Eroded
dates yield
no parentheses of time.
Squirrels' nails catch
on tree bark as they
spiral upward in chase;
crows idle
on branches high above,
signals the dead would
understand if they
had ears to listen.

Salt of the Earth

> *Why do clouds cry so much*
> *growing happier and happier?*
> *Neruda*

With each proffered drop of rain,
sky shouts to cathedrals of salt:
Arise from stained faces and
bless all the earthen tombs.

How is it that saline
never extends
its portion of tears
as an offering?

Hands Full of Heaven

How many churches
are there in heaven?
Neruda

In a child's finger play,
hands back-side-up with fingers
interlaced, knuckles entwined—
except for the steeple
where first fingers touch and point
upward, assuming that *up*
is superior to *down*—

people wait behind closed doors.
If no one opens them,
how will we know
if any communicants
are kneeling on padded benches
awaiting God's presence
in bread and wine?

What of other congregations
that do not kneel in worship
or don't know *Heaven Came Down*,
others that seek to restore Babel's tower?
Will their stained windows
keep out clouds of doctrine
and showers of theology?

Cycle of Tears

How do we thank the clouds
for their fleeting abundance?
            Neruda

Eons of our bottled tears, kept
for just this use, accumulate in the air
until shakers of tiny salt grains
dry inside. We empty our shakers
onto the soil with the sweat of futility—
pray for the anointing of our land.
Clouds cry in their travail, overcome
rivers of labor and flood the land.
Old and new bottles overflow
with the joy of clear sky while
generations drown in hunger—
our bodies once afloat together
with the tides, now whitened bones
strewn across a dusty new sea.

Beneath Occluded Shine

Where did the full moon leave
its sack of flour tonight?
Neruda

In the gently tugged tide
lies the leaven.
See bubbles erupt
along the surface?
Tonight renders excess,
a final call for all revenants.

Meditation on Prayer

Is it true our desires
must be watered with dew?
Neruda

The blessing of night lies
upon the greenery of the ground.
We beg for this,
pray that our wants
become those of Divinity.
As each drop of dew
passes into atmosphere,
want becomes need,
a less than divine addiction
with neither hope of withdrawal
nor substitute.

Rose

When is the appointment of the rose
decreed under the earth?
Neruda

Petals
over the linked
chain—their rusted jailor—
sail down, cover clover. Color
pelts. Rain
sieges.
The gardener shakes each prismed drop.
On the other side, no
guardian waits
for sun.

Family History

Why do trees conceal
the splendor of their roots?
Neruda

One oak climbed skyward
more than one hundred years
before burial with its roots.

A hollowed willow suffered
heart rot, until it could
no longer thirst nor bend.

A maple's bark curls and peels.
Trunk exposed, time will erode
the depths of each root's tendrils.

White anchors, unprotected,
mirror vacant branches above.

Marzanna

Cannot a kiss of spring
also kill you?
        Neruda

From the birch leaves yellowing
till the willows begin to green,
what passes between
is a bitter record
of repeated retreat.
And you are the steward
of the splendid remains
until—at your consent—
children burn then drown
you, a sacrifice to spring.

Afterlife Landscape

Why does the professor teach
the geography of death?
            Neruda

When the heart muscle renders life flat
and the body leaves linear reality,
what topography will be encountered
before the pyre of ablated horizons?

Denizens

What is it that upsets the volcanoes
that spit fire, cold and rage?
                    Neruda

You are the temperature
too hot not to be cold,
surging from the core,
circulating the flow of a fury
churned to dizziness.

You swallow a mountain,
spew the lava of our folly.
We settle on the cold scheme
of this cemented surface,
we, your new inhabitants.

The Physics of Flight

> *Why don't the immense airplanes*
> *fly around with their children?*
> Neruda

Lift and thrust do not apply
to the invisible. Heft matters
more to children dragged
in the thin chaos of escape.

Fright

> *From what does the hummingbird*
> *hang its dazzling symmetry?*
> Neruda

Consider the hummingbird
stuck in the shed when lightning whips,
how thunder speeds the flight to nowhere.

Envy

What does old ash say
when it passes near fire?
                    Neruda

O to manifest that radiant flare!
To combust again as poems become
kindling! There must always be
remnants of verse—pulp
burned to warm our bodies—ash
to be captured on the wind.

Smoke and Cloud

Does smoke talk
with the clouds?
                Neruda

From fireplaces and foundries,
forests bereft of foliage,
crack houses abandoned but full,
trains aflame off their tracks,
roofs stabbed by lightning,
smoke's ashy arms stretch
beyond pillows of vapor
then shrug back into the soft
embrace of cloud.

Smoke speaks nothing of this
sacrifice for the sake of ethereal
communion in submission to the force
that would douse its origins but
which chooses instead escape.

Notes

Epigraphs are taken from *Book of Questions* by Pablo Neruda.

In "Hands Full of Heaven," "Heaven Came Down" is the abbreviated title of the Gospel hymn by John W. Peterson.

A line from "Marzanna" was suggested by Wanda Schubmehl.

Marzanna is the Polish folk representation of winter, symbolically burned and thrown in the river at a festival each spring.

Claudia M. Stanek holds an MFA from The Writing Seminars at Bennington College. Her chapbook, *Language You Refuse to Learn*, was a co-winner of Bright Hill Press's 2013 annual contest. Claudia's poems have been published in *Cutleaf, Ekstasis, Solum, Book of Matches,* and *Atticus Review.* Her work has also been anthologized in *Like Light: 25 Years of Poetry & Prose* by Bright Hill Press, several issues of *Le Mot Juste,* and the *Tennessee Voices Anthology.* Her poem "Housewife" was selected by Judith Lang Zaimont for a commissioned libretto for the Eastman School of Music's Women in Music Festival. Claudia received a writer's residency in Poland, where her work was translated into Polish. She is a founding member of poetry non-profit Just Poets (Rochester, NY). She now lives in East Tennessee where her life is managed by her rescued dogs.

www.ingramcontent.com/pod-product-compliance
Lightning Source LLC
Chambersburg PA
CBHW030053100426
42734CB00038B/1543